I see plainly that you're a selfish.

Rupert Brooke (1887—1915)
English poet

ex hara producte.
Ex-tenant of a pig-sty.

Cicero (106—43 BC)
Roman orator, statesman and philosopher
from *In Pisonem*

Until I breathe my final breath,
the only peace we will declare
Will be the kind that exists
Between the wolves and the
defenceless sheep.

Ovid (43 BC—c. AD 18)
Roman poet, from *Ibis*

I do frown on thee with all my heart,
And if mine eyes can wound, now let them kill thee.

William Shakespeare (1564—1616)
English poet and playwright
from *As You Like It*

Thou foul, filthy cabbage-head.

Aphra Behn (1640—89)
English novelist, playwright, poet, translator and spy
from *False Count*, 1682

Every body may be damned, as they seem fond of it,
and resolved to stickle lustily for endless brimstone.

George Gordon, Lord Byron (1788—1824)
English poet

Vous yourself!

Cruel stony hearted wretch,
snatcher of bread from a starving child ...

George Bernard Shaw (1856—1950), Irish playwright, from a letter to English actress
Mrs Patrick Campbell, February 27th, 1913.

iniuria es.
You are iniquity
incarnate.

Plautus (c. 250—184 BC)
Roman comic playwright
from *Miles Gloriosus*

Published in 2003 by
Chicago Review Press, Incorporated
814 North Franklin Street
Chicago, Illinois 60610

ISBN 1-55652-514-1

Designed by Sarah Allen Cruz and Michelle Lovric
Concept and compilation copyright © 2002 Michelle Lovric
Editorial Assistant: Kristina Blagojevitch
Printed in Thailand by Imago

0 9 8 7 6 5 4 3 2 1

ACKNOWLEDGMENTS

extracts from letters by George Bernard Shaw to Mrs Patrick Campbell reprinted courtesy of the Trustees of Mrs Patrick Campbell deceased.

extracts from *The Book of Ghastly Curses* by Elizabeth St. George, published by Spook Enterprises. Copyright © Spook Enterprises, 1982, 1996. With special thanks to Elizabeth St. George for her help.

extracts from *ARAE, The Curse Poetry of Antiquity* by Lindsay C. Watson, published by Francis Cairns (Publications) Limited. Copyright © Lindsay C. Watson, 1991.

For him that steals or borrows and returns not this book, let it change into a serpent in his hand and rend him. Let him be struck with palsy and all his members blasted ... Let bookworms gnaw his entrails in the token of the Worm that dieth not ...

Scribal curse in a bible from the Monastery of San Pedro, Barcelona, Spain.

The Insult & Curse Book

compiled by Michelle Lovric

Arrant, malmsey-nose knave!

William Shakespeare
from *Henry IV Part 2*

CHICAGO REVIEW PRESS

Dost thou jeer and flout me in the teeth?
William Shakespeare (1564—1616) English poet and playwright, from *The Comedy of Errors*

Speak the truth but then clear out quickly. Serbian proverb

CONTENTS

INSULTS & JIBES

THREATS & IMPRECATIONS

Less than Human

Exchange between the English playwright
Douglas Jerrold and a fellow diner,
who held up a piece of meat on his fork, asking:

"Is this pig?"

6

Jerrold's
reply: **"To which end of the fork do you refer?"**

Bestial Comparisons

Thou debosh'd fish, thou!

William Shakespeare (1564—1616)
English poet and playwright
from *The Tempest*

There never lived a viler viper upon the face of the earth than thou.

Sir Edward Coke (1552—1634), English jurist, to Sir Walter Raleigh at the latter's trial for treason.

7

Scorpionem prae morum acritudine vulgus appellat.
The people call him the Scorpion, on account of his poisonous personality.

Apuleius (b. c. 123)
Latin writer
from *Metamorphoses*

A lamentably successful cross between a fox and hog.

James G. Blaine (1830—93)
American journalist and politician,
on American soldier Benjamin Franklin Butler.

Thou ugly, filthy camel's face.

Elizabeth, Queen of Bohemia (1596—1662)
to James Hay, Earl of Carlyle.

8

You're the victim
of a sleaze story
to the effect that
a rutting goat
is lodged in your
armpit.

Catullus (c. 84—54 BC)
Roman poet

**Thy impudence hath a
monstrous beauty
like the hindquarters
of an elephant.**

James Elroy Flecker (1884—1915)
English poet and playwright

I class him among infidel wasps and venomous insects.

James Boswell (1740—95)
Scottish biographer, on English
historian Edward Gibbon.

Thackeray settled like a meat-fly on whatever one had got for dinner, and made one sick of it.

John Ruskin (1819—1900)
English writer, artist,
designer and philosopher

I had as lief be wooed of a snail.

William Shakespeare (1564—1616)
English poet and playwright
from *As You Like It*

Farting insect!

Japanese insult

9

Those eyebrows wound up looking like African caterpillars!

Bette Davis (1908—89)
American actress, on her great
rival Joan Crawford.

larva
Incubus!
Plautus (c. 250—184 BC)
Roman comic playwright

You starveling, you eel-skin, you dried neat's tongue, you bull's-pizzle, you stock-fish ...

William Shakespeare (1564—1616)
English poet and playwright
from *Henry IV Part 1*

The stink emanating from the brackish swamp,
... or the antediluvian stench of a salt-water pond,
or a musty old goat panting over his nanny,
or the old boot of a dog-tired ex-soldier,
... or the halitosis of miserable defendants in the dock,
or the sputtering oil-lamp of perverted Leda,
... or a fox in flight, or a viper's lair,
I'd rather smell of any of these,
Bassa, than smell of you.

Martial (c. 40—103), Roman poet, from *Epigrams*

10

More kid in him than
a goat in the family way!

Rough as goat's knees.

Australian expressions

...choragus of his
Bulgarian tribe of
autocoprophagous
baboons, who make
the filth they feed on.

Algernon Swinburne (1837—1909), English poet
from a letter to American writer Ralph Waldo
Emerson, 1874. Emerson had allegedly called
Swinburne "a mere sodomite".

A cheeky comment made by a young man to an old lady driving a herd of beasts:

"Good morning, mother of asses!"

11

Her reply: # "Good morning, son!"
A fragment from the ancient Greek

**Why dost thou converse with that trunk of humours,
that bolting-hutch of beastliness, that swollen parcel of dropsies,
that huge bombard of sack, that stuffed cloak-back of guts,
that roasted Manningtree ox with the pudding in his belly ...**

William Shakespeare (1564—1616), English poet and playwright, from *Henry IV Part 1*

You haven't got the brains of a bandicoot.

Australian insult

12

You whoreson upright rabbit!

William Shakespeare (1564—1616)
English poet and playwright
from *Henry IV Part 2*

You blankety-blank,
flop-eared,
sheep-headed
coyote

O. Henry (1862—1910)
American writer

She sounds more and more like Donald Duck.

Bette Davis (1908—89), on fellow American actress Katharine Hepburn.

She has the face of an exhausted gnu.

John Simon, American critic,
on American actress Anjelica Huston.

A dilapidated macaw ...

Edith Sitwell (1877—1964)
English poet, on English woman of
letters Lady Mary Wortley Montagu.

... the spawn of an adder.

Martin Luther (1483—1546)
German religious reformer,
on King Henry VIII of England.

She has the bear's ethereal grace.

Lewis Carroll (Charles Dodgson) (1832—98)
English mathematician and writer

... the face, with the long
proboscis, the protruding teeth
of the Apocalyptic horse ...

George Meredith (1828—1909), English novelist and poet,
on English writer George Eliot.

**He's so low he can't kiss
a tumblebug's gilliewinkie
without bending his knees.**

Contemporary slang

Charles R. Thorne, American actor
to Rose Eytinge, his leading lady, who yawned at
the climax of one of his anecdotes:

"For heaven's sake, Rose, don't swallow me!"
Her response: **"You forget, Mr Thorne, that I am a Jewess."**

**Weak as a mouse
fallen into gingelly oil!**
Badaga insult, India

15

The rankest sow in town!

American John Porter describing his mother;
he was jailed in 1664 for calling his father
a "Liar, and simple Ape".

Braindead

The jelly-boned swine,
the slimy, the belly-wriggling invertebrates,
the miserable sodding rotters, the flaming
sods, the snivelling, dribbling, dithering,
palsied, pulseless lot that make up England today.

D. H. Lawrence (1885—1930), English writer,
on the Englishmen who did not
appreciate his work.

Dumb & Dumber

More of your conversation would infect my brain.
William Shakespeare (1564—1616)
English poet and playwright
from *Coriolanus*

You have a 1/2-horsepower brain, pulling a two-ton mouth.
Anonymous writer to Richard Meltzer, American journalist and critic, who had published a critical article about English musician Paul McCartney.

17

Bless your pointed little head!
American college slang for intellectuals.

You must have had a very vulgar education.
John Gay (1685—1732)
English playwright and poet

I wish I had known you when you were alive.
L. L. Levinson (1905—74), American writer

You buffle-headed stupid creature you!
William Wycherley (1640?—1716)
English playwright

COWCAT!

A person whose main function is to occupy space. An insignificant or negligible personality.
Frank Gelett Burgess (1866—1951) American humorist and novelist

BARMY FROTH!

An empty light-headed person.
16th-century English insult

This dodipoule, this didopper ...

Thomas Nashe (1567—1601)
English playwright, on English
poet Gabriel Harvey.

18

Unmitigated noodles!

Kaiser Wilhelm II (1859—1941), German Emperor and King of Prussia, on the English.

You shall follow me, you Avicenna, Galen, you gentlemen of Paris, Montpellier, Germany, Belgium and Vienna ... None shall stay in a corner and have the dogs urinate at him — all shall follow me, and the monarchy of medicine shall be mine. This dirt you shall eat! All the universities and all the old writers put together are less talented than my rear end.

Theophrastus Bombastus von Hohenheim (Paracelsus), 16th-century German physician and chemist, to all his enemies, both living and dead, in the medical profession.

Contemporary Slang

A Kangaroo loose in the top paddock

As bright as a bump on a log

Just fallen off the turnip truck

Not wrapped too tight

Bone from the knees up!

Dorkus Malorkus (plural Dorki Malorki)

Inhabitant of Moron Manor

Strudel brain

Twenty-minute egg

Parmecium brain

Pencil sharpener repairman

Seems to have taken a few whacks from the stupid stick

The clue meter is reading zero

Crazy Mojo the African weasel

Contemporary slang

Elle a une araignée au plafond!

She has a spider on her ceiling!

French slang for a foolish woman.

A hyena that wrote poetry in tombs.

Friedrich Nietzsche (1844—1900), German philosopher, on Italian poet Dante Alighieri.

A louse in the locks of literature.

Alfred, Lord Tennyson (1809—92), English poet, on English critic John Churton Collins.

20

He was simply a hole in the air.

George Orwell (1903—50) English novelist, on English politician Stanley Baldwin.

A vacuum with nipples.

Otto Preminger (1906—86) Austrian-born American film director, on American actress Marilyn Monroe.

Meredith is, to me, chiefly a stink.

Ezra Pound (1885—1972) American poet and critic, on English writer George Meredith.

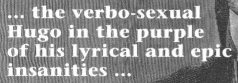

... the verbo-sexual Hugo in the purple of his lyrical and epic insanities ...

François Daudet, 20th-century French critic, on French writer Victor Hugo.

The bubonic plagiarist.

Jonathan Miller (b. 1934), English doctor and director, on English television personality David Frost.

He chews more than he bites off.

Clover Adams (1843—85) on fellow American writer Henry James.

... the great fecal Zola, celebrant at the altar of the Supreme Filth ...

François Daudet, 20th-century French critic, on French writer Emile Zola.

He has not so much brain as ear-wax.

William Shakespeare (1564—1616)
English poet and playwright
from *Troilus and Cressida*

This book of essays ... has all the depth and glitter of a worn dime.

Dorothy Parker (1893—1967), American writer, on English writer Margot Asquith's *Lay Sermons*. Parker also declared that Asquith "reverts to tripe" in the book.

Sir Walter Scott (when all's said and done) is an inspired butler.

William Hazlitt (1778—1830)
English writer

22

His mind was a kind of extinct sulphur-pit, and gave out nothing but a smell of rotten sulphur.

Thomas Carlyle (1795—1881), Scottish historian, on French Emperor Napoleon III.

Begotten of froth out of foam.

Herbert Asquith (1852—1928), on fellow English politician Winston Churchill.

His mind was like a Roquefort cheese, so ripe that it was palpably falling to pieces.

Van Wyck Brooks (1886—1963), American author and critic, on English writer Ford Madox Ford.

Never did I see such apparatus got ready for thinking, and so little thought.

Thomas Carlyle (1795—1881), Scottish historian, on English poet Samuel Taylor Coleridge.

23

I know that he is more of a windbag than the industrial rawhide bellows used in factories where rocks are melted down to make iron.

Plautus (c. 250—184 BC), Roman comic playwright, from *Mnesilochus*

Drags on like cow's saliva.

Japanese insult

24

E. M. Forster never gets any further than warming the teapot.

Katherine Mansfield (1888—1923), New Zealand-born writer, on English writer E. M. Forster.

There can be no kernel in this light nut; the soul of this man is his clothes.

William Shakespeare (1564—1616)
English poet and playwright
from *All's Well That Ends Well*

With the single exception of Homer, there is no eminent writer, not even Sir Walter Scott, whom I can despise so entirely as I despise Shakespeare when I measure my mind against his. The intensity of my impatience with him occasionally reaches such a pitch, that it would positively be a relief to me to dig him up and throw stones at him ...

George Bernard Shaw (1856—1950), Irish playwright

His intellect is of no more use than a pistol packed in the bottom of a trunk if one were attacked in the robber-infested Apennines.

Prince Albert (1819—61)
Consort to Queen Victoria,
on their son, the future Edward VII.

His brain is as dry as the remainder biscuit after a voyage.

William Shakespeare (1564—1616), English poet
and playwright, from *As You Like It*

25

Fricassée of dead dog.

Thomas Carlyle (1795—1881), Scottish historian, on English writer Monkton Milnes' *Life of Keats*.

The triumph of sugar over diabetes ...

George Nathan (1882—1958), American essayist, on the works of J. M. Barrie, Scottish creator of *Peter Pan*.

She writes like a man in petticoats, or a woman in breeches.

Mary Russell Mitford (1787—1855), English novelist and playwright, on the English writer Hannah More, from a letter to her friend, Mrs Hofland, October 6th, 1820.

Retorts

Baloney!
Balderdash!
Applesauce!
Banana oil!
Bunkum!

Contemporary slang

Cowyard confetti!
Meadow Mayonnaise!
Rubbish!

Australian expressions

Horsecollar!

American military slang, meaning rubbish, Second World War.

You're talking Fanny Nanny.
All My Eye and Betty Martin!

Naval expressions signifying disbelief; the second one is believed to derive
from an excuse that a sailor entering a Catholic Church had merely sung the
hymn "Mihi Beate Martine".

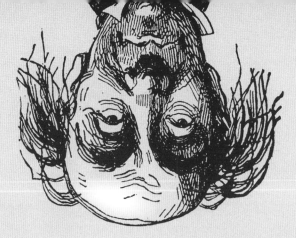

The Midwife laid her hand on his Thick Skull,
With this Prophetick blessing — *Be thou dull*.
John Dryden (1631—1700), English poet, on English playwright Thomas Shadwell.

[You are] duller than a great thaw.
William Shakespeare (1564—1616), English poet and playwright, from *Much Ado About Nothing*

Thou has displayed an utter absence of education, thou
dragger of dead dogs from obscure gutters.
James Elroy Flecker (1884—1915), English poet and playwright

You have a head, and so has a Pin.
Jonathan Swift (1667—1745), Irish writer

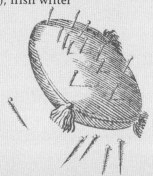

Mome, malthorse, capon, coxcomb, idiot, patch!

William Shakespeare (1564—1616)
English poet and playwright
from *The Comedy of Errors*

No good to Gundybluey.

Australian expression, meaning useless.

Thou Puff of Bad Paste!

Anonymous, on English actor and
writer Samuel Foote (1720—77).

GRIZZLE-DEMUNDY! Laughing fool, who grins at everything.

Francis Grose (1731?—91)
English antiquary and lexicographer
from *A Provincial Glossary*, 1787

DICKED IN THE NOB!

Silly. Crazed.

NIGMENOG!

A very silly fellow.

NOCKY BOY!

A dull simple lad.

all from *The Classical Dictionary
of the Vulgar Tongue*, 1785

29

On seeing a friend's first short story, English actor and playwright Noël Coward told her:

"Frankly my dear, I should bury it in a drawer and put a lily on it."

Exchange between the English poet William Wordsworth and writer Charles Lamb:
Wordsworth:

30

"I believe that I could write like Shakespeare, if I had a mind to try it."

Lamb:

"Yes, nothing wanting but the mind."

I have only been mildly bored.

Gertrude Atherton (1857—1948), American novelist, to Ambrose Bierce, after an argument of fierce literary debate.

A female cellist auditioning for the English conductor Sir Thomas Beecham finished her first piece and asked him:

"What shall I do next?" His reply: **"Get married."**

I like your opera. One day I think I'll set it to music.
Richard Wagner (1813—83), German composer, to an unfortunate young composer.

I had a wonderful evening, but this wasn't it.
Groucho Marx (1895—1977), American actor, to his hostess, on leaving a Hollywood party.

On entering a room during a sudden silence, English poet Samuel Rogers (1763—1855) observed: Henry Hallam was an English historian.

"I see that Hallam has just been telling a joke."

Your mouth is
puckered and
looks like
a heap of
house dust.

Yoruba insult, Nigeria

32

**Deformed Sir, The Ugly Club in full meeting have elected you an
honorary Member of the Hood-Favoured Fraternity. Prince Harry was
lean, Falstaff was fat, Thersities was hunchbacked, and Slowkenlergus
was renowned for the eminent miscalculation which Nature had
made in the length of the nose; but it remained for you to unite all
species of deformity and stand forth the Prince of Ugly Fellows.**

Letter to American President Abraham Lincoln from one of his citizens.

Old & Ugly

You have killed a baboon and stole his face.

from *The Classical Dictionary of the Vulgar Tongue*, 1785

I never forget a face, but in your case I'm willing to make an exception.

Groucho Marx (1895—1977), American actor,
to a woman who complained he had forgotten meeting her.

He was so ugly he hurt my feelings.

Jackie "Moms" Mabley (1894—1975)
American singer and comedian

He reminds me of nothing so much as a dead fish before it has had time to stiffen.

George Orwell (1903—50), English novelist, on English politician Clement Attlee.

She had a face on her that'd fade flowers.

34

George Ade (1866—1944)
American humorist and playwright

Now to me, Edith looks like something that would eat her young.

Dorothy Parker (1893—1967)
American writer

If he were a horse, nobody would buy him ...

Walter Bagehot (1826—77)
English economist and
journalist, on English
politician Lord Brougham
and Vaux.

I have seen better-looking faces on pirate flags.

Anonymous on English politician
Alec Douglas-Home.

A plumber's idea of Cleopatra.

W. C. Fields (1879—1946), American actor, on American actress Mae West.

**... their faces looked ... as if they
were raked out of hel, and sent
into the world by great Beelzebub,
to terrifie and astonish mortall men ...**

Thomas Coryat (c. 1577—1617), English traveller,
on the Egyptian population of Nevers.

Belly-god
Big Mama Gonga Gonga
Gutling
Hyperthyroid Pukeathon
Lumbering bohunkus
Pancake nipple
Tub of guts
Frankenstein's
monster's babushka

Contemporary slang

GUNDIGUTS!

A fat, pursy fellow.

GOTCH-GUTTED!

Pot-bellied: a gotch in Norfolk
signifying a pitcher, or large round jug.

MR DOUBLE TRIPE!

A fat man.

TRIPES AND TRULLIBUBS

the entrails; also, a jeering appellation for a fat man.

all from *The Classical Dictionary of the Vulgar Tongue*, 1785

Your mother has a protruding navel!

Japanese taunt

... flabby, fat, and flatulent looking ...

John Norton (1858—1916)
English writer, on Queen Victoria.

Miss United Dairies herself.

David Niven (1910—83)
British actor, on American
actress Jayne Mansfield.

He waddles like an Armenian bride.

Osmanli saying

Your roly-poly jelly-belly sticks out a foot and a half in front of you.

Persius (34—62)
Roman satirist
from *Satire*

37

I have never liked bargains when it came to sex.

Hedy Lamarr (1913—2000)
Austrian-American actress

Clueless & Loveless

**Your virginity,
your old virginity,
is like one of our
French wither'd pears:
it looks ill, it eats drily.**

William Shakespeare (1564—1616)
English poet and playwright, from *All's Well That Ends Well*

Cat's tits!

Japanese insult for
a poorly endowed girl.

The 18th-century French writer Madame de Staël longed to be beautiful and loved to be told that she was. Fishing for compliments, she once asked French statesman Talleyrand to choose whether he would save her or a well-known beauty from drowning.

He replied, bowing: **"Oh Madame, you swim so well."**

Henry VIII, on seeing his fourth wife, Anne of Cleves, for the first time:
"You have sent me a Flanders mare."
The marriage was never consummated.

Exchange between Edna Ferber, American novelist, and Noël Coward, English actor and playwright, who met one day in New York, wearing similar suits:

Coward: **"Edna, you look almost like a man."**

Ferber: **"So do you."**

The languid way in which he gives you a handful of numb unresponsive fingers is very significant.

Thomas Carlyle (1795—1881), Scottish historian, on English poet William Wordsworth.

He's nothing more than a basin of octopus.

A Venetian expression used to describe an old man who believes he has the kind of sexual capacity on which, in his case, the sun has now set.

40

Platonic pimp of all posterity!

George Gordon, Lord Byron (1788—1824), English poet, on Petrarch.
from *Don Juan*

George Gordon, Lord Byron

Thou foul, filthy cabbage-head
Aphra Behn

Go and drink with the flies!
Australian expression

schoenobates
Low-life trapeze-artist!
Juvenal

Thou debosh'd fish, thou!
William Shakespeare

Away, you cutpurse rascal, you filthy bung, away!
William Shakespeare

May all the **goats** in Gorey chase you to

Hell

Irish curse

May you live in *interesting* times!

Chinese curse

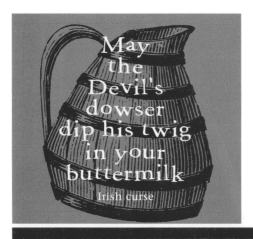

May the Devil's dowser dip his twig in your buttermilk

Irish curse

Thou Ugly, Filthy Camel's Face

Elizabeth, Queen of Bohemia

Hit Your Head on a corner of tofu and Die!

Japanese curse

The Pus of a poxy fox on your Whisky

Irish curse

May you wander forever in the company of crashing literary bores

And be afflicted with the world's worst case of piles.

Priapea 41

May the Cats eat your women

Irish curse

Pox, Piles and a heavy vengeance!

English curse

I wish I had known you when you were alive

L. L. Levinson

lutulente
Dirt-bag!
Cicero

**Of all the past,
present and future
fatheads, idiots,
imbeciles, mushrooms,
morons, hare-brains
and
chipmunk-cheeks ...**
Plautus

You
have
killed
a
baboon
and
stole
his
face.

I have never
liked bargains
when it came
to sex.
Hedy Lamarr

I'll have you
stuffed and
mounted.

Japanese
threat

18th-century
insult

That kiss is comfortless
As frozen water to a starved snake.
William Shakespeare (1564—1616)
English poet and playwright, from *Titus Andronicus*

Roe-deer would sooner mate with Apulian
wolves (than I would sleep with you).
Horace (65—8 BC)
Roman poet, from *Odes*

You say all the girls are on fire for you?
***You*, with a face like a man swimming**
under water?
Martial (c. 40—103)
Roman poet

41

Überdork
Un-shagalicious
Contemporary slang

Badly Behaved

'Tis a vice to know him
William Shakespeare (1564—1616)
English poet and playwright
from *Hamlet*

schoenobates
Low-life trapeze-artist!
Juvenal (fl. early 2nd century)
Roman satirist, from *Satire*

lutulente
Dirt-bag!
Cicero (106—43 BC)
Roman orator, statesman and
philosopher, from *In Pisonem*

42

**BEARD-SPLITTER!
MUTTON-MONGER!**
A man addicted to wenching.
from *The Classical Dictionary of the
Vulgar Tongue*, 1785

... one that converses
more with the buttock
of the night than with the
forehead of the morning.
William Shakespeare (1564—1616)
English poet and playwright
from *Coriolanus*

Naughty & Not Nice

43

Exchange between the
Earl of Sandwich and politician John Wilkes:

Sandwich:

"Sir, you will die either of the pox or on the gallows."

Wilkes:

"That depends on whether I embrace your lordship's mistress or your principles."

His crimes are the only great thing about him..

Richard Brinsley Sheridan (1751—1816), Irish playwright, on British colonial administrator Warren Hastings, who had been charged with corruption in India.

You had to stand in line to hate him.

Hedda Hopper (1890—1966), American gossip columnist, on American film producer Harry Cohn.

A one-man slum.

Unattributed description of American journalist Heywood Campbell Broun (1888—1939).

You should cross yourself when you say his name.

Marlene Dietrich (1904—92), German-born American actress, on Orson Welles.

44

He hardly drinks tea without a stratagem.

Samuel Johnson (1709—84), English writer and critic, on English poet Alexander Pope.

He lies like a French bulletin.

Dutch saying

He's a most notable coward, an infinite and endless liar, an hourly promise-breaker, the owner of no one good quality.

William Shakespeare (1564—1616), English poet and playwright, from *All's Well That Ends Well*

He can lie out of both sides of his mouth at the same time ...

Harry S. Truman (1884—1972), on fellow American politician Richard Nixon.

Liar! lying lips, lying eyes, lying hands, promise breaker, cheat, confidence-trickster!

George Bernard Shaw (1856—1950), Irish playwright, from a letter to English actress Mrs Patrick Campbell, August 12th, 1913.

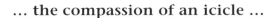

... the compassion of an icicle ...

S. J. Perelman (1904—79), American writer, on American actor Groucho Marx.

Spongy eyes, and a supple conscience ...

Colonel Edward Saxby, once a supporter of Oliver Cromwell, quarrelled with him and demanded that he should be assassinated. This comes from a pamphlet he published in 1657, describing his foe.

On hearing that English politician Randolph Churchill (1911—68) had undergone surgery, writer Evelyn Waugh commented:

"A triumph of modern science to find the only part of Randolph that wasn't malignant and remove it."

So mean he wouldn't spit on a burnt hand!

Badaga insult, India

When he leaves our house let us count our spoons.

Samuel Johnson (1709—84)
English writer and critic

Bludger!

Australian expression for someone who idly sponges off others.

Away, you cutpurse rascal, you filthy bung, away!

William Shakespeare (1564—1616)
English poet and playwright
from *Henry IV Part 2*

Low-down hootchie-cootcher.

A "lurker-about", from the song "Minnie the Moocher" by Cab Calloway, 1931.

... field-butcher, land-pirate.

Harper's Weekly on American president Abraham Lincoln.

Have you eaten goat recently?

Irish insult, referring to Saint Patrick's pet,
which was eaten while he was meditating.

You're muckson up to the Huckson.

Dirty up to the knuckles.
Francis Grose (1731?—91)
English antiquary and lexicographer
from *A Provincial Glossary*, 1787

47

Her soul was like some quaggy latrine into which every imaginable iniquity had flowed.

Apuleius (b. c. 123)
Latin writer
from *Metamorphoses*

Never have I seen a more shameless degree of libertinism ... she wallowed and floundered in vice as if it were her natural element.

Maxime du Camp, 19th-century French writer, on the beautiful French courtesan Ludovica Pradier.

48 *puella defututa*
A thoroughly tried and tested nymphomaniac.

Catullus (c. 84—54 BC)
Roman poet

... bedroom habits little better than a mink's.

Mae West (1892—1980)
American actress

I haven't had as many affairs as Joan Crawford — but outside of a cat house, who has?

Bette Davis (1908—89), American actress, on her great rival.

49

Why, thou arrant butter whore, thou cotqueane and scrattop of scoldes ...
Thomas Nashe (1567—1601), English playwright,
on English poet Gabriel Harvey.

VORIANDER!

A woman who pursues men,
especially when she is unattractive.
Frank Gelett Burgess (1866—1951)
American humorist and novelist

He's the dummy headman of an extinct village.

Badaga insult for someone who puts on airs, India.

She hath been to London to call a strea a straw, and a waw a wall.

A Cheshire insult, said of a person who puts on airs and returns from the big city refusing to speak the local dialect any longer. Francis Grose (1731?—91), English antiquary and lexicographer from *A Provincial Glossary*, 1787

50 Was there a star in the East when this self-worshipping little man was born?

Jean Rook (1931—91), English journalist, on Eric Morley, organizer of the Miss World competition.

Full of Hot Air

Poor man, he's completely unspoiled by failure.

Noël Coward (1899—1973), English actor and playwright, on a fellow playwright.

If a traveller were informed that such a man was the leader of the House of Commons, he might begin to comprehend how the Egyptians worshipped an ant.

Benjamin Disraeli (1804—81), English politician and novelist, on the Whig leader Lord John Russell.

He is the great father of all the "I! I! I!'s" of all the I-dolators ...

François Daudet, 20th-century French critic, on French statesman the Vicomte de Chateaubriand.

Mr Whistler has always spelt art with a capital "I".

Oscar Wilde (1854—1900), Irish playwright, on American artist James McNeill Whistler (who gave as good as he got, accusing Wilde of recycling the witticisms of others).

Declarations of War

See here, you slack-salted, transubstantiated interdigital germarium, you rantipole sacrosciatic rock-barnacle — if you give me any more of your caprantipolene paragastular megalopteric jacitation, I'll make a lamel-libranchiate gymnomixine lepidopteroid out of you!

Frank Gelett Burgess (1866—1951)
American humorist and novelist

You scullion! Your rampallian! You fustilarian! I'll tickle your catastrophe!

William Shakespeare (1564—1616), English poet and playwright, from *Henry IV Part 2*

I'll have you upstairs and downstairs ...

Catullus (c. 84—54 BC), Roman poet

I'll have you stuffed and mounted.

Japanese threat

Your kind puts mine in jail for violent assault on authority. My kind makes the living language. Your kind preserves the language my kind makes. Your kind and mine are always at war.

Jack London (1876—1916), American novelist, from a letter to V. C. Gilman, a literary critic who had found fault with London's language.

NO, I AM NOT DEAD, AND I WOULD LIKE TO IMPRINT PROOF OF MY UNEQUIVOCAL EXISTENCE ON YOUR SHOULDERS WITH A VERY VIGOROUS STICK. I WOULD DO SO, IN FACT, DID I NOT FEAR THE PLAGUE MIASMA OF YOUR MEPHITIC CORPSE

Marquis de Sade (1740—1814), French writer, from a letter to a columnist for the journal *Ami des Lois*, 1799. The columnist had published a premature obituary for the Marquis in which he condemned his sexually explicit work *Justine*.

Shakespearean Threats

If I were but two hours younger I'd beat thee.
from *All's Well That Ends Well*

I will knog your urinal about your knave's cogscomb ...
from *The Merry Wives of Windsor*

[I'll] make a quagmire of your mingled brains.
from *Henry VI Part 1*

I shall shake thy bones out of thy garments.
from *Coriolanus*

You would answer very well to a whipping.
from *All's Well That Ends Well*

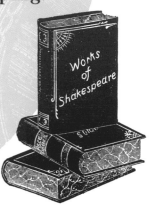

18th-Century Slang

I WILL ANOINT YOU WITH THE OIL OF GLADNESS!
Ironic threat, meaning I will beat you.

I'LL PROMISE YOU A LUSHING MUZZLE!
Naval term, meaning a blow on the mouth.

I'LL CRACK YOUR NAPPER!
I'll break your head!

I'LL GIVE YOU A CLOUT ON YOUR JOLLY NOB!
I'll give you a blow on your head!

I WILL KNOCK OUT TWO OF YOUR EIGHT EYES!
A common Billingsgate threat from one fish nymph to another: every woman, according to the naturalists of that society, having eight eyes:— viz. two seeing eyes, two bub-eyes, a bell-eye, two pope's eyes, and a * * *-eye. He has fallen down; and trod upon his eye; said of one who has a black eye.

I'LL THRIPPA THEE!
I'll cudgel you.

I'LL GIVE YOU A CORNISH HUG!
A Cornish threat: this is a wrestling grip.

I'LL LET OUT YOUR PUDDINGS!
I'll slit your stomach and let your guts fall out ...

55

May their bodies be cursed.
May they be cursed in the head and the brain.
May they be cursed in their eyes and their foreheads.
May they be cursed in their ears and their noses.
May they be cursed in fields and in pastures.
May they be cursed in the mouth and the throat,
cursed in the chest and the heart,
cursed in the stomach, cursed in the blood,
cursed in the hands and feet and in
each of their members.
May they be cursed going in and going out.
May they be cursed in towns and in castles.
May they be cursed in streets and in squares.
May they be cursed when sleeping and when awake,
when going out and returning,
when eating and drinking,
when speaking and being silent.
May they be cursed in all places and at all times.

56 Excommunication curse found at the Abbey of Fécamp,
founded by Duke Richard I of Normandy in 990.

He will crush out your blood, and make
it fly, and it shall be sprinkled on His
garments, so as to stain all His raiment.
He will not only hate you, but He will
have you in the utmost contempt; no
place shall be fit for you but under
His feet to be trodden down as the
mire of the streets.

From a sermon by Jonathan Edwards
(1703—58), American preacher, whose
rantings were said to have led to
depression and even suicide in
members of his congregation.

Toads, beetles, bats, light on you!

William Shakespeare (1564—1616)
English poet and playwright
from *The Tempest*

May you live in interesting times!
Chinese curse

nec tibi sol calidus.

For you, may the sun never be warm.
Ovid (43 BC—c. AD 18), Roman poet, from *Ibis*

May your whole village be covered with grass!
Badaga curse, India

You should grow like an onion,
with your head in the sand!
Jewish curse

You lie in the way of strushins!
You are on the path to destruction.

Francis Grose (1731?—91)
English antiquary and lexicographer
from *A Provincial Glossary*, 1787

Boils and plaques
Plaster you o'er, that you may be abhorr'd
Farther than seen, and one infect another
Against the wind a mile!

William Shakespeare (1564—1616)
English poet and playwright, from *Coriolanus*

May the great gripes settle on thee!

James Elroy Flecker (1884—1915)
English poet and playwright

Hope you get the Barcoo Vomit.

Australian expression, referring to a bush sickness.

May the meat and drink go up and down
in your bellies as men go to harrow.

Alice Skilling, cursing the local minister and churchwardens, 1608.

May beets grow
in your navel so
you piss borscht!
Yiddish curse

Pox, piles and a
heavy vengeance!
16th- and 17th-century English curse

May you spend your
days burning tarred
rope in a bucket and
squatting on it.
Irish curse, referring to a cure for piles.

May you wander forever
in the company of
crashing literary bores
And be afflicted with the
world's worst case of piles.
Priapea 41

59

EGYPTIAN
PILE CURE
...
...RS. ROEBUCK & CO.
...CAGO

I'd like to see you abject, scorned, and despised by all others, a creature of self-despair and self-loathing, peering anxiously at everything, trembling at every little noise, having given up on your own affairs, without words, without liberty, without power ... a quaking, shivering sycophant.

Cicero (106—43 BC), Roman orator, statesman and philosopher, from *In Pisonem*

Go and drink with the flies!

Australian expression, meaning go and drink alone.

May hippos dance upon your roof and make it most unwaterproof.
May bats within your attic rest, may mewlips come, your house infest.
May alligators on the stair repeat a doleful cry "beware".
May kangaroos in dreadful fright keep all thy house awake at night.
May corkscrews bent with evil guile strip down thy bathroom tile by tile.
While in the kitchen warthogs three do scare the tanin from your tea.
Now in your lounge a snake will dance
and comment on your circumstance.
May crowds of emus on your lawn
let fireworks off to greet the dawn,
Whilst thirty walrus in the hall
enjoy a game of basketball.
If you desire to end
this curse,
invite me back
lest things get
worse.

Laughter Curse
from *The Book of
Ghastly Curses*

60

Irish Household Curses

May the devil's dowser dip
his twig to your buttermilk.

May the cats eat your women!
An Irish beggar's curse on an ungenerous household.

The pus of a poxy fox in your whiskey.

Six eggs to you and a half-dozen of them rotten.

May your hens take the disorder (the fowl-pest),
your cows the crippen (phosphorosis),
and your calves the white scour!
May yourself go stone-blind so that you will not
know your wife from a haystack!

May the man who would curse the bladder out of
a goat have a chat with you before Christmas.

Zodiac Curse

Spin, O wheel of the skies in this, the midnight hour. As thou dost spin, let my curses spin to the blackness. Before all these stars, witness my word of power.

May the earth of the Sea Goat open beneath him. By the stars of **Capricorn**, let him be trampled into dust and scattered through the dark clouds of the nebulae.

May the bolt of fire from the Archer stun him from the heavens. By the glitter of **Sagittarius**, let him be rained upon by flames and scalded by meteoric spears.

May the sting of the scorpion lodge in his heart and may Antares savage his mind with a terrible fear. By the icy power of **Scorpio**, may the void overtake him.

May the scales weigh him in justice, in the air of **Libra**. By the balance of Libra, let the dark winds blow his soul unto infinity.

May the maiden turn from him in unbelief. By the beauty of **Virgo**, let him be deserted of earth and may he walk the way of chaos. Let chaos take him until itself.

May the roar of the lion strike terror unto his heart. May **Leo** stalk him by night and day. By the light of Regulus and in the glare of the sun, before the power and the strength burn him to nothingness.

May the crab reach for him with claws of fear. May the steady star of **Cancer** flood him with illusion, worse than the phantoms of the moon.

May the twins deafen him with their chatter. May the glory of **Gemini** divide him completely, that the celestial tempest is heard in his mind.

May the bull make the earth open to swallow him up. May **Taurus** gore his body and may Aldebarren light his way to the silence of the grave.

May the ram burn him with a terrible force of destruction. May **Aries** burn him with a terrible burst of cosmic flame within the furnace at the heart of a star.

May the fish bring a flood to wash away all memory and trace of him. May **Pisces** engulf him in the waters of darkness.

May the waterman take him to interstellar void. Before **Aquarius** and in the star Formalhaut, let him be scattered.

O stars of the zodiac, witness these, my words of power.
Let my curse spin into the blackness as thou dost spin.
Turn, oh wheel of the skies, turn and destroy him forever.

Zodiac Curse from *The Book of Ghastly Curses*

If you rub me out, I will slander you to Euripides. Keep off.

Manuscript curse appended to a papyrus of Homer's *Iliad*, 1st to 3rd century BC.

I am going to scrawl filth about you over the whole wall of the wine-shop.

Catullus (c. 84—54 BC), Roman poet

God (who cannot lie) hath threatened that his curse shall never depart from the house of the Swearers ... and I doubt not but you are already cursed, though you know it not; that either he hath cursed you in your body by sending you some foul Disease; or in your estate, by suddenly consuming it, or in your name, by blemishing and blasting it; or in your seed, by not prospering it, or in your mind, by darkening it, or in your heart, by hardening it, or in your conscience, by terrifying it ...

Richard Younge (fl. 1640—70), English writer of Calvinist tracts, from *A hopefull way to Cure that horrid Sinne of Swearing*, c. 1644

64

... may he have upon him much seaweed from the sea-scum, and may his teeth rattle, as he lies like a dog helpless and face down just where the waves break.

Ancient Greek tomb curse, known as the Strasbourg Epode.

... for him may the thinkable become unthinkable, the easy difficult, practical aims unachievable, the productive unproductive, the corn fields barren, the fertile infertile, the sweet bitter, the fortunate unfortunate, the bright dark, the happy full of grief, and birthdays a matter of grief.

Ancient tomb curse, against robbers, Salamis, Cyprus.
Both from *ARAE, The Curse Poetry of Antiquity*, 1991, by Lindsay Watson

Death and bad luck afterwards to you.

Irish curse

66

I shall consider you dead until the day that prostitute's body which resembles yours dies.

Jean Mounet-Sully (1841—1916), French actor, to his lover, Sarah Bernhardt, July 9th, 1875.

The devil swallow him sideways!

Irish curse

Morto ti, mi pianzo un dì.
If you die, I'll cry for a day.
Venetian proverb

You pretend to die, and
I'll pretend to bury you.
Creole proverb

The fate of Ned's cock to you!

Irish curse to a vain person. Ned's cock
fell in love with its reflection in a pond,
fell into the water and drowned.

Here's a quarter.
Call someone who cares.
Contemporary American expression

*non ego tuam empsim
vitam vitiosa nuce.*
Your life's not worth a rotten nut to me.
Plautus (c. 250—184 BC) Roman comic playwright, from *Miles Gloriosus*

May the sky over them be made of brass and the earth underfoot of iron so that the heavens will be unable to receive their souls and earth unable to receive their bodies.

Excommunication curse found at the Abbey of Fécamp, founded by Duke Richard I of Normany in 990.

68

God damn your god damned old hellfired god damned soul to hell and god damn you and god damn your god damned family's god damned hellfired god damned soul to hell and good damnation god damn them and god damn your god damn friends to hell.

Letter to American President Abraham Lincoln from a disgruntled citizen.

... when his time comes I shall buy a piece of the rope for a keepsake.

Mark Twain (1835—1910), American writer, on South African politician Cecil Rhodes.

I'LL SEE YOU KICKERAPOO!
I'll see you dead.

from *The Classical Dictionary of the Vulgar Tongue*, 1785

Hit your head on a corner of tofu and die!
Japanese curse

Let the sharks of the sea rend his flesh.
Let the kraken consume his bones. Let
him be lost in the waters, the restless
waters that permit no peace. In the name
of the water, so let it be done.

Water curse
from *The Book of Ghastly Curses*

69

**May you be torn in strips and have a rag
for a bonnet.**

Irish curse

Irish Curses

May all the goats in
Gorey chase you to hell!

To Death and smothering upon you!

The death of the kittens
(i.e. drowning) upon you!

Six horse-loads of graveyard clay on top of you!

May you be mangled!

May the seven terriers of hell sit on the spool
of your breast and bark in at your soul case!

Let vultures vile seize his lungs.

William Shakespeare (1564—1616), English poet and
playwright, from *Henry IV Part 2*

**[Whoever removes this stone]
may Bel and Shamash tear out his
foundation and exterminate his posterity.**

Temple curse in Nippur, Babylon, c. 3800 BC.

**Let him be fried in a pan; let the falling sickness and
the fever seize him; let him be broken on a wheel, and hanged.
Amen.**

Scribal curse in a 12th-century bible from Arnstein Abbey, Germany.

**Lie heavy on him, earth! for he
Laid many heavy loads on thee.**

Dr Abel Evans (1679—1737), English clergyman and epigrammatist
A mock epitaph for the playwright and architect Sir John Vanbrugh,
who built Blenheim Palace.

Hanging's Too Good

YOUR COLQUARRON IS JUST ABOUT TO BE TWISTED!
You're about to be be hanged.

YOU'LL BE DANCING UPON NOTHING.
You'll be hanged.

YOU'LL BE FRUMMAGEMMED!
Choked, strangled, suffocated, or hanged.

YOU WILL HAVE A HEARTY CHOAK AND CAPER SAUCE FOR BREAKFAST!
You will be hanged.

All from *The Classical Dictionary of the Vulgar Tongue*, 1785

YOU'LL BE MADE TO WALK UP LADDER LANE AND DOWN HEMP STREET!
Naval expression, threatening hanging at the yard arm.

Go forth and gather you the soul of my enemy to take
him to the place of darkness. Thy lair, O lord of the
underworld. Cipactli, may he hear the beat of thy
heart to inspire him with terror. Cipactli, may he hear
the clash of thy jaws and see thy teeth in the darkness.
May he hear the whiplash of thy tail as he encounters
thee. In terror shall he expire as thy jaws close upon
him to take him below the water. Thus shall it be
done, Cipactli! Cipactli! Cipactli!

South American prayer to the evil alligator god.
from *The Book of Ghastly Curses*

If you die from fright, your soul will be farting.

Serbian curse

When you are dying, may insects make holes in you!

Badaga curse, India

Suppose that your old age were to be cut short
By the popular vote on grounds of your depravity,
I get the feeling that your tongue,
rolled up in lies, would be cut out,
and thrown to a vulture;
a crow would slit your eyes
and suck them down his black throat,
dogs would crunch your guts
and wolves would gnaw the left-overs.

Catullus (c. 84—54 BC)
Roman poet

THE APPARITION

When by thy scorne, O murdresse, I am dead,
And that thou thinkst thee free
From all solicitation from mee,
Then shall my ghost come to thy bed,
And thee, fain'd vestall, in worse armes shall see;
Then thy sicke taper will begin to winke,
And he, whose thou art then, being tyr'd before,
Will, if thou stirre, or pinch to wake him, thinke
 Thou call'st for more,
And in false sleepe will from thee shrinke,
And then poore Aspen wretch, neglected thou
Bath'd in a cold quicksilver sweat wilt lye
 A veryer ghost than I;
What I will say, I will not tell thee now,
Lest that preserve thee: and since my love is spent,
I had rather thou shoudst painfully repent,
Than by my threatnings rest still innocent.

John Donne (1572—1631)
English cleric and poet

74

You're going to become a pathetic old hag,
Weeping over callous paramours in some
deserted alley.

Horace (65—8 BC), Roman poet, from *Odes*

**Cur, you will pay
the wages of sin!**

Virgil (70—19 BC), Roman poet
from *Aeneid*

May a
consumptive
cobbler castrate
you on a
red-hot last.

Irish curse

**Look at this lovely little
pearl-handled revolver I saw in
a gunsmith's shop, the other day.
It is engraved with the motto:
"Si je t'aime, garde à toi!"**

(If I love you, look out for yourself!)
Frank Gelett Burgess (1866—1951)
American humorist and novelist

Rain screams on her!

Catullus (c. 84—54 BC), Roman poet

Thy lips rot off!

William Shakespeare (1564—1616)
English poet and playwright
from *Timon of Athens*

May the French ulcer love you and the Lord hate you!

Arabian curse
French ulcer is a sexual disease.

May you have the runs on your wedding night.

Irish curse

Morning screams to you.

Irish marriage curse

Carnality and concupiscence, out of control and wild as mares on heat, shall carouse about your fevered organs.

Horace (65—8 BC), Roman poet, from *Odes*

... Fancy the rut of the lash to blush
Your sweet flanks and soft buttocks?
You'll gyrate like a toy boat
Caught out at sea in a wind grown
wild with adult pain.
Catullus (c. 84—54 BC), Roman poet

Lamp, if thou are a god, take
vengeance upon the deceitful
girl. When she has a friend
within, and is sporting
with him, go and give
them no more light.
Asclepiades (fl. 1st century BC)
Greek physician

May hound-wounding, heart-
ache, and vultures gouging her
eyes, Derangement and madness
on her mind come soon!
May the entrails and mansion of
pleasure out of this worm fall out!
But may she still be alive till
everyone's sick at the sight!
Peadar O Dior'n, 18th-century Irish poet, cursing the
lover who rejected him.

Should anyone feel the urge to mess with my girl,
May Love incinerate him in the barren mountains.
Grafitti, Pompeii

77

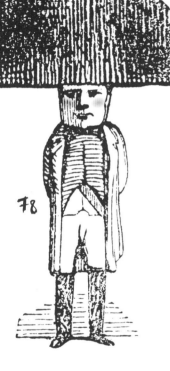

I love you no longer; on the contrary, I detest you. You are a wretch, truly perverse, truly stupid, a real Cinderella. You never write to me at all, you do not love your husband; you know the pleasure that your letters give him yet you cannot even manage to write him half a dozen lines, dashed off in a moment! What then do you do all day, Madame? What business is so vital that it robs you of the time to write to your faithful lover? What attachment can be stifling and pushing aside the love, the tender and constant love which you promised him? Who can this wonderful new lover be who takes up your every moment, rules your days and prevents you from devoting your attention to your husband? Beware, Josephine; one fine night the doors will be broken down and there I shall be.

Napoleon Bonaparte (1769—1821), French emperor, from a letter to his wife, Josephine, 1797.

When I think that you are being untrue to me with women, I have murder in my heart.

Aline Bernstein (1914—72), American writer, from a letter to American novelist Thomas Wolfe, August 11th, 1928.

I will scratch the word love out of my dictionary.

Captain James Hackman, 18th-century English clergyman, from a letter to Martha Reay, mistress of the Earl of Sandwich, March 26th, 1776. He eventually shot her and was executed for her murder.

God send my enemies a celibate life.

Ovid (43 BC—c. AD 18), Roman poet, from *Amores*

May thy emissions never exist.

Egyptian curse from *The Book of Ghastly Curses*

79

You have forgotten
But the Gods remember
And so does the Truth
It's the Truth which
will make you sorry
One Day
For everything you did,
and everything you do.

Catullus (c. 84—54 BC)
Roman poet

Anti-terrorist curse

In the name of the scarlet one, the crimson one, the one
of strength and justice. In his name do we call.

I will stand in the place of bloodstone and ruby.
I will come to the place of garnets and carbuncles.
I will call upon the one who wields the scarlet flame of justice.

Grant to us justice and strength.

This is the place of swords and shields. This is the place where
fire is fed with the blood of men, the tears of women and the
flesh of the conquered kings.

Grant to us justice and strength.

This is the place where the boars have crimson fangs.
This is the place where the elephants are ankleted with the skulls
of conquered kings. This is the place of the serpents who lick up
cities and civilisations.

Grant to us justice and strength.

This is the place where the clashing of swords is heard, the scream
of the dagger, the falling of walls and the cries of the conquered.

Grant to us justice and strength.

Hear our curse those who have done this thing. They have
brought terror to the innocent. They have wrought destruction
with no warning. O Destroyer of Opposition, may these men
come before the sword of justice. Thy retribution is without
passion. Cleanse this world of their corruption.

Grant to us justice and strength.

May they know of terror. May they be accursed.

Adapted from a Babylonian curse by Elizabeth St. George.

80

foetorem extremae latrinae.

You are the stench of a low-life latrine.

Apuleius (b. c. 123)
Latin writer
from *Metamorphoses*

I have begun to scorn your scorn …

Lady Mary Wortley Montagu (1689—1762)
English woman of letters

You mean those clothes of hers are intentional?

Dorothy Parker (1893—1967)
American writer

The very pimple of the age's humbug.

Nathaniel Hawthorne (1804-64), American writer,
on English writer Edward Bulwer-Lytton.

Why do you sit there looking like
an envelope without any address on it?

Mark Twain (1835—1910)
American writer

*furiosissimum atque
egentissimum ganeonem.*

Most rabid and extravagant debauchee!

Cicero (106—43 BC)
Roman orator,
statesman and
philosopher
from *Pro Sestio*

You call me vous.

Napoleon Bonaparte (1769—1821), French emperor,
from a letter to his wife, Josephine, 1796.

You're enough to try the patience of an oyster.

Lewis Carroll (1832—98)
English mathematician and writer